MR. NUTS AND MR. BALLS

RICHARD P. WEINER

There were many people I wished to thank
for helping me with the creation of this book.
For some reason, none of them wanted
to be publicly acknowledged.

ISBN 978-1-939298-20-1
ISBN 978-1-939298-21-8

For more information please DO NOT contact
Three Flowers Press
P.O. Box 2833
Chapel Hill, 27515-2833
www.threeflowerspress.com

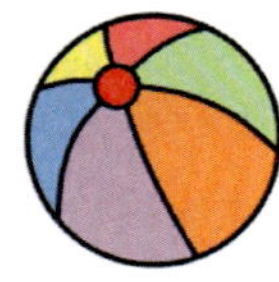

**For my mother,
my son's sixth grade teacher,
and the old lady in the parking lot.**

Hello, I'm Mr. Nuts!

You've got to be kidding.

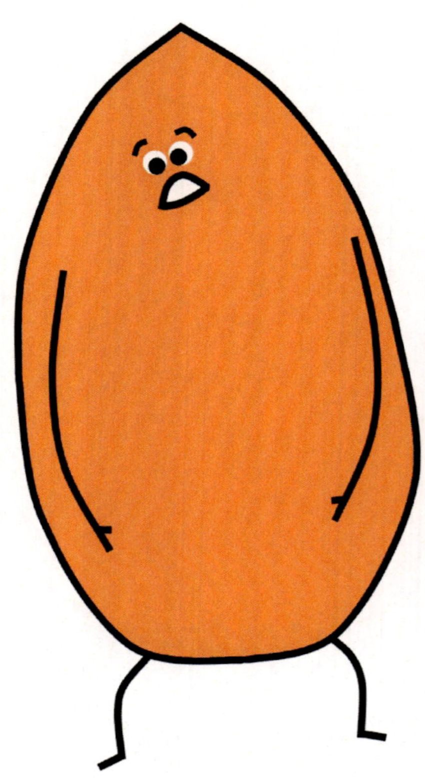

Why, what's your name?

Mr. Balls.

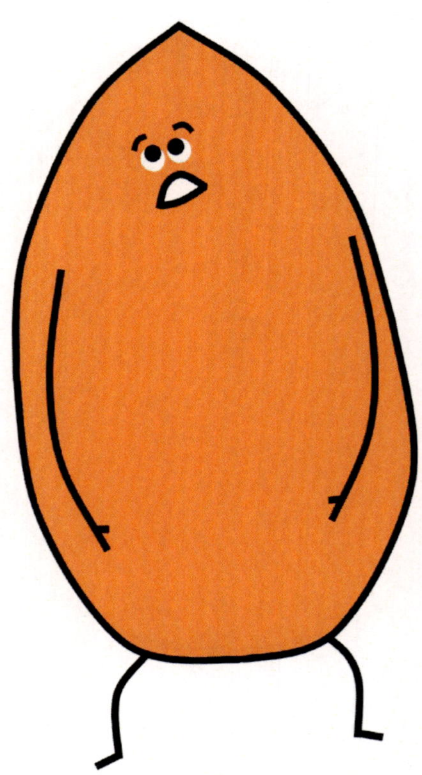

Oh, like that's any better.

Of course it's better.
Balls beat nuts any day of the week.

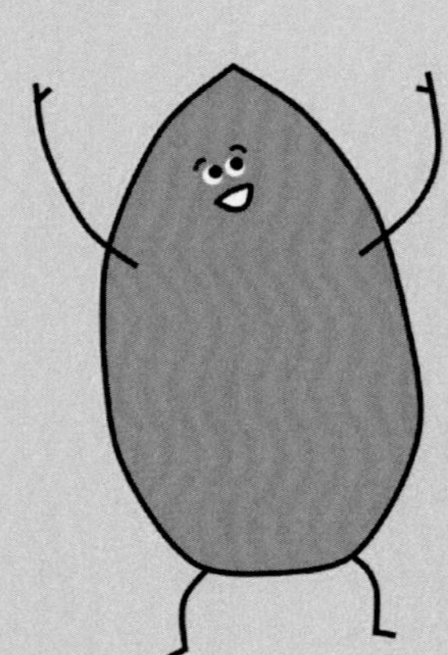

Don't be ridiculous. Nuts are delicious! No one wants to eat balls.

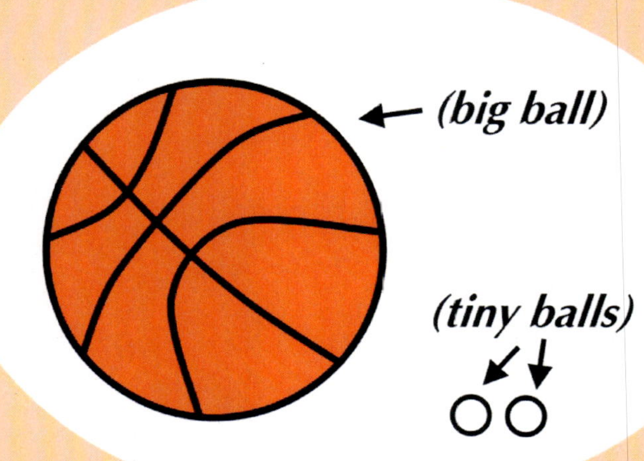

Maybe not,
but you can play with
balls. And they can be as big as
basketballs or as tiny as ping pong balls.
Nuts are all the same size: small.

**Untrue.
Coconuts are quite large.
And hairy!**

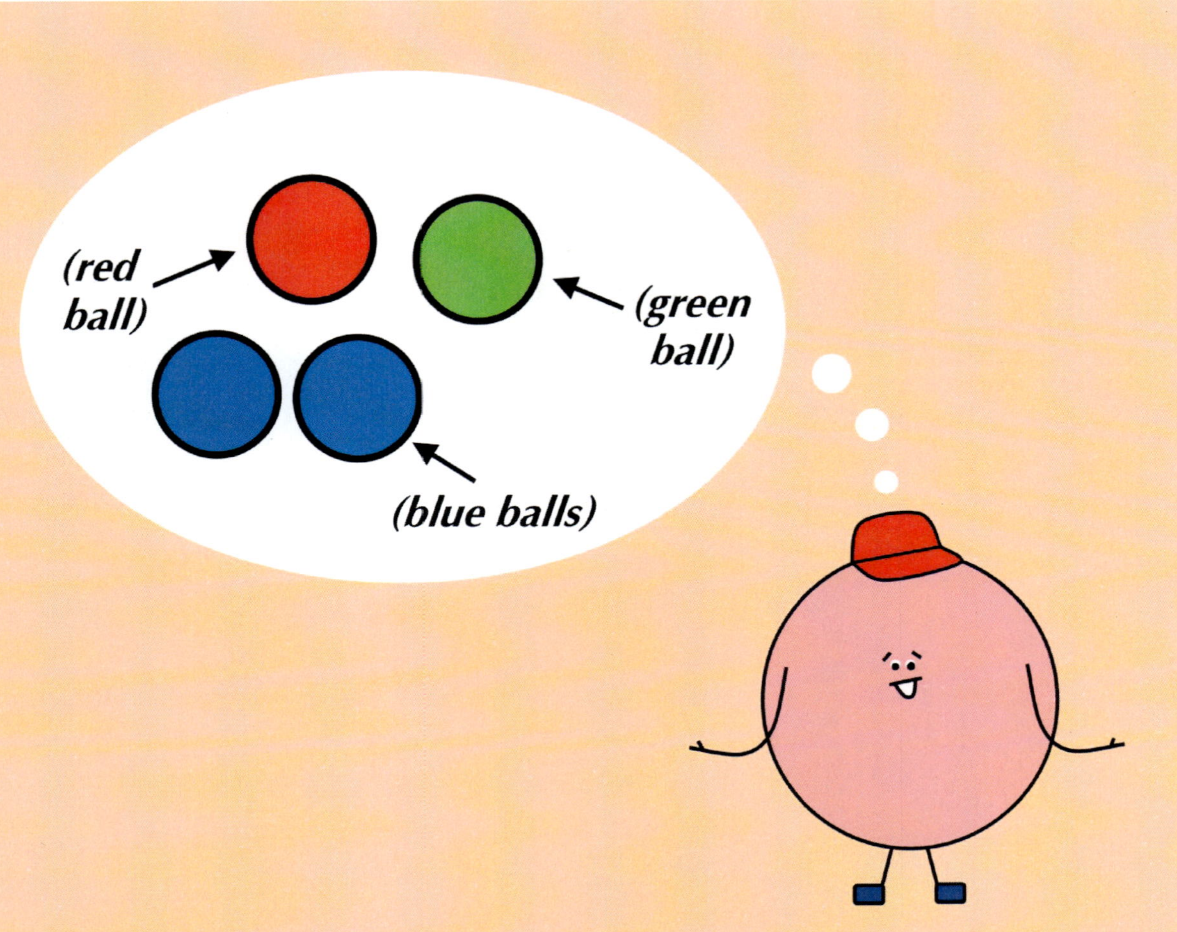

Hairy-schmary, they're boring. Balls come in tons of colors. Nuts are always the same dull color: brown.

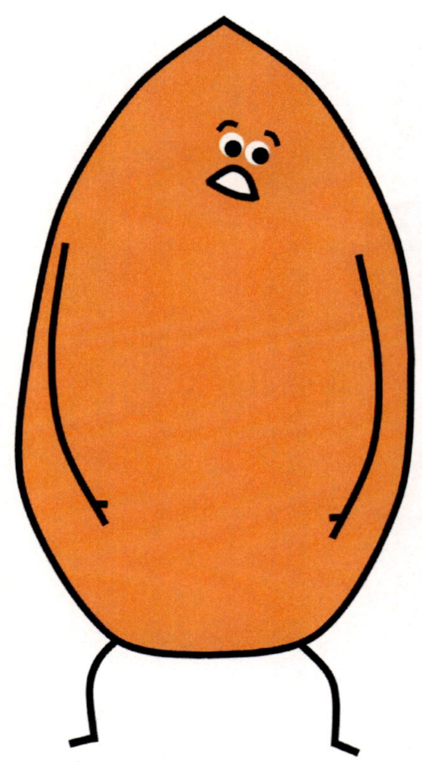

Nuts are brown because they come from the earth. They are natural and nutritious. Who doesn't like a nice, salty nut?

Anyone who's allergic, that's who. Have you ever heard of anyone allergic to balls?

That's only because balls aren't natural. Most are probably made of rubber or nasty plastic.

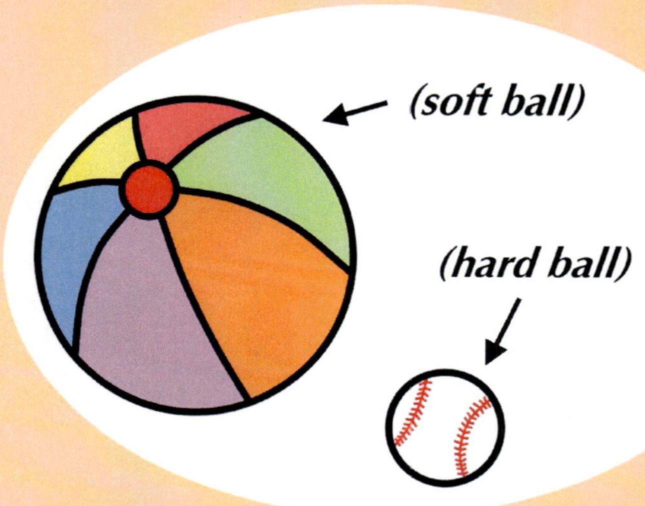

**But plastic is
what gives balls their amazing
variety! That's why they can be soft
like beach balls or hard like baseballs.**

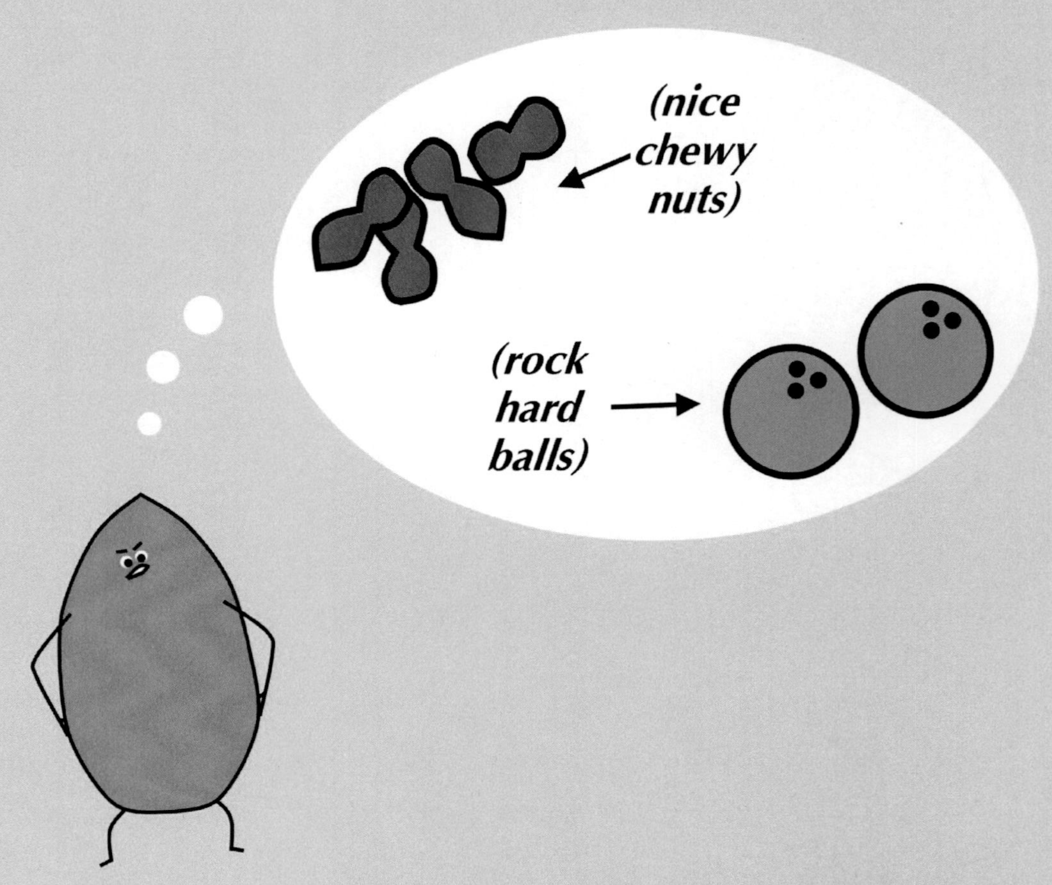

And nuts can be chewy or crunchy. I, for one, would rather have some nice chewy nuts than rock hard balls.

**Oh yeah?
Those nuts might
be chewy now, but in a
few years they'll be dried and shriveled.
Nothing nastier than a sack of old nuts.**

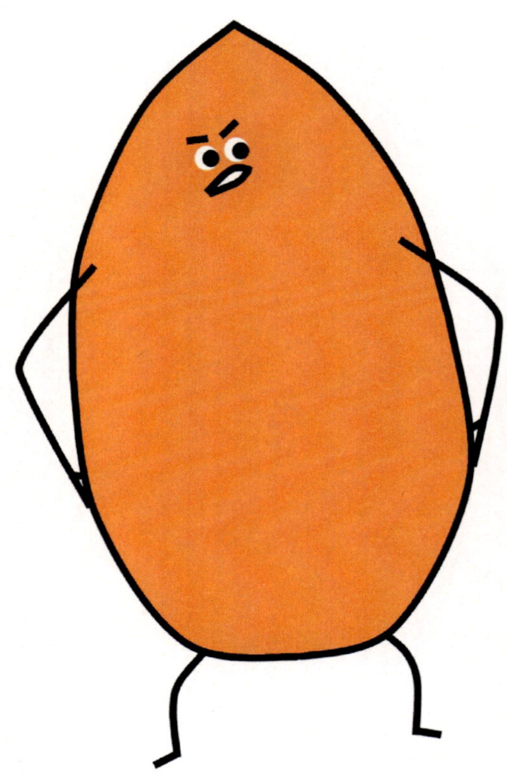

That's it.
We need to settle this once and for all.

Agreed.

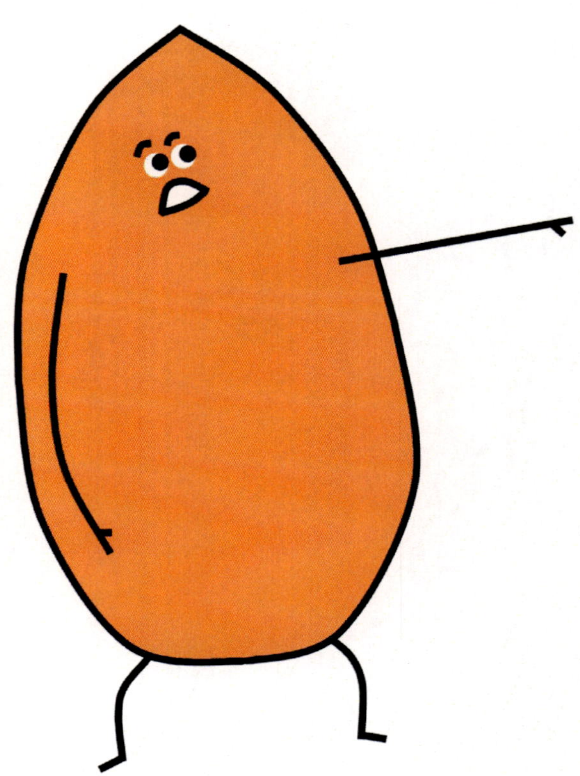

Let's ask that guy over there.

**Yeah, let's do it.
Hey you, what's your name?**

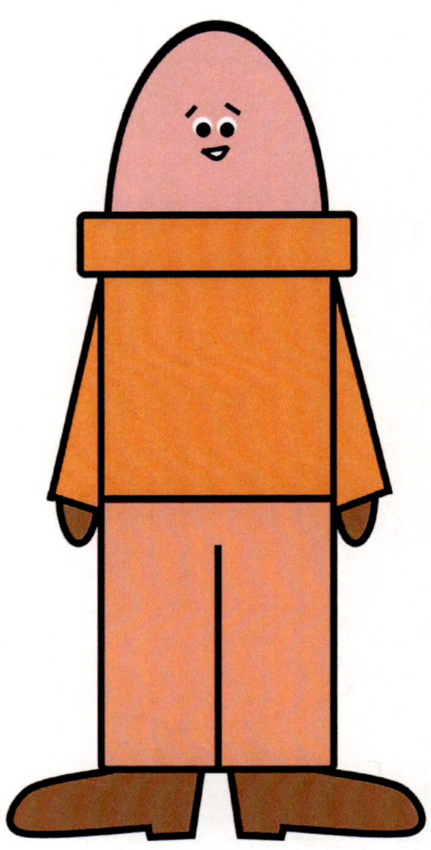

I'm Mr. Dick!

Made in the USA
San Bernardino, CA
04 December 2014